KATRINA

8 HOURS THAT CHANGED
THE MISSISSIPPI COAST FOREVER

A SURVIVOR

A message was written on a rooftop in Pass Christian, Miss., by a Hurricane Katrina survivor to let his relatives know he was safe. This neighborhood was pulverized by the storm. DAVID PURDY

Katrina - 8 Hours That Changed the Mississippi Coast Forever

Editors: Keith Chrostowski, Kansas City Star; Drew Tarter and Dorothy Wilson, Sun Herald

Designer: Kelly Ludwig, The Ludwig Agency Inc.
Written by Kat Bergeron, Mike Lacy, Anita Lee, Jim Mashek, Ricky Mathews, John McFarland, Stan Tiner, David Tortorano, Dorothy Wilson, Sun Herald

Sun Herald photo staff: James Edward Bates, John C. Fitzhugh, Tim Isbell, and David Purdy, staff photographers; Drew Tarter, photo director

Special thanks to the following contributing photographers:
Nick Oza, Macon Telegraph
Patrick Schneider, Charlotte Observer
Brandi Jade Thomas, St. Paul Pioneer Press
Al Diaz, The Miami Herald
Chris Stanfield, St. Paul Pioneer Press
Jared Lazarus, The Miami Herald
Chris Ochsner, The Kansas City Star
Mark Cornelison, Lexington Herald-Leader
Mike Cardew, Akron Beacon Journal
Karl Mondon, Contra Costa Times
Brian Blanco, Bradenton Herald
Mike Yacksyzn II, Biloxi, Miss., resident

Technical support: Gretchen O'Boyle, The Sun Herald

Copyright © 2005 The Sun Herald, Biloxi, Miss.
No part of this book may be reproduced, stored in a retrieval system, or transmitted in any form or by any means electronic, mechanical, photocopying, recording or otherwise, without the prior consent of the publisher.

Published by The Sun Herald, Biloxi, Miss.

First edition.

ISBN 10: 1-933466-09-X
ISBN 13: 978-1-933466-09-5

Printed in the United States of America by Walsworth Publishing Co., Marceline, Missouri

To order copies, call 1-800-591-2097.

Order on-line at www.SunHerald.com.

COVER: FAITH ALIVE

Bambi Battise and her son, Glenn Battise, 1, survived Katrina but lost their home. "God does test us. We go through trials every day. I'm not going to lose my faith," she says. NICK OZA

KATRINA
8 HOURS THAT CHANGED THE MISSISSIPPI COAST FOREVER

FROM THE RUBBLE, A NEW SOUTH MISSISSIPPI IS BORN

Hurricane Katrina was an equal opportunity destroyer. The storm swept away beautiful beachfront mansions along with modest cottages far from the shore. It destroyed the smallest of small businesses and devastated the largest employers along the Mississippi Gulf Coast.

This book reflects what South Mississippi was like before Katrina stormed ashore on Monday, Aug. 29, 2005, what Katrina's winds and storm surge did to South Mississippi that day, and what South Mississippians immediately began doing to cope with and recover from this unprecedented natural disaster.

Much of this book acknowledges the tremendous loss inflicted on the communities of South Mississippi by Katrina. But South Mississippians are determined that Katrina will not have the last word in this story.

This book closes with a celebration of the survival and renewal of South Mississippi.

It contains not only the work – in words and photographs – of the Sun Herald's dedicated staff, but also the work of journalists from many other Knight Ridder newspapers who rushed here to help tell this unparalleled story.

Their labors have captured the wonderful spirit and incredible resilience of the people and of what was – and will be again – one of the most vibrant places to live in America.

Ricky Mathews
Publisher
Sun Herald
South Mississippi's Newspaper

LOOKING AT WHAT'S LEFT

Residents of Second Street in Gulfport, Miss., walk through the wasteland that used to be their neighborhood. The street, laden with renovated cottages and older homes, was one of Gulfport's nicest residential areas. JOHN C. FITZHUGH

SOUTH MISSISSIPPI: A GULF COAST JEWEL

By David Tortorano and Dorothy P. Wilson

Time and again whenever people talked about the state's economy, they'd say the engine was South Mississippi.

It was home to three of the state's Top 5 employers, with more than $3.3 billion in new commercial and industrial development under way. It had seen a 25 percent growth in new jobs and a doubling of retail sales since 1995.

South Mississippi was a magnet for tourists, the builder of tools for the nation's defense and, in more recent years, a hotbed for research. It was listed in Forbes as a "Top 100 Places to Do Business" and in Money magazine's "Best Places to Live" survey.

Indeed, we had entered a boom with no end in sight. The Coast's strong economy and job growth were expected to propel the population from 364,000 in 2000 to nearly 400,000 this year.

Instead, this year brought Hurricane Katrina.

Of course, we WILL recover. And even as we continue to wring our hands a little and dig out from the disaster, there are already indications that the boom will continue, just in a different way.

Before Katrina, South Mississippi's economy stood on several pillars, including

CASINO ROW

Casinos arrived on the Mississippi Coast in 1992, when those who saw them as an economic boost overcame a mixed vote. The law dictated they must be on the water so the giant gambling barges, more like buildings than anything headed down an industrial canal, naturally settled in areas that had once catered to seafood processors and canners. For the most part, that's the case here on Casino Row on Biloxi's Point Cadet. JOHN C. FITZHUGH

MILITARY MIGHT

Airmen from Keesler Air Force Base in Biloxi begin a Parade of Heroes by carrying 50 American flags. The base is a major South Mississippi employer.
TIM ISBELL

retailing, major industry, tourism and a big federal presence.

Because South Mississippi touches the shoreline, tourists had always visited. But in the early 1990s with the advent of casinos, they began coming in droves. Hotels opened by the dozens and other tourist-oriented operations blossomed.

Before Katrina, a dozen casinos floated along the bays and Mississippi Sound, sporting championship golf courses and yacht-filled marinas and drawing top-name entertainment. The tourism industry had hit the $3 billion revenue mark and was attracting more than 11 million visitors yearly.

South Mississippi's federal presence is defined by defense contractors like shipbuilding giant Northrop Grumman. But there are also aerospace and advanced weaponry companies. Northrop Grumman runs two shipbuilding operations, one in Gulfport and the

other in Pascagoula. Other big players, including VT Halter Marine, dot the region.

The defense segment also includes a growing aerospace industry, with the most notable new addition being Northrop Grumman's unmanned aerial vehicle plant in Moss Point.

In the advanced weaponry field, General Dynamics has an operation in Stone County that builds rockets. And at the John C. Stennis Space Center, defense contractor Ionatron is establishing a facility to build laser-based weapons systems.

Other key players are Keesler Air Force Base and Air National Guard and Naval Construction Battalion bases. Wages to personnel and the services provided to the bases by private contractors ripple through the local economy.

Before Katrina, South Mississippi's economy also was growing in the more usual ways. More than $1.3

billion in new projects, including relocations and expansions by 20 companies, had been announced before the hurricane. Distribution, marine fabrication, deep-water offshore drilling rig construction and polymer/chemical processing plants were seeing the most dramatic growth.

More than $90 million had been invested in new health-care facilities including one new hospital, a new medical mall and several outpatient facilities and medical office buildings.

In more recent years, the construction trades were expanding, thanks to rapid condominium growth and the housing boom. And the advanced materials segment and the "knowledge" industry, which includes research by federal and university units, were taking off.

Now what? That's the question everyone's asking.

Already, it's obvious that construction will emerge as one of the big dogs in the new South Mississippi economy. Houses, condos, churches, schools, hospitals and businesses need to be rebuilt.

The casinos will come back — more opulent and on land instead of on the water, safer from hurricanes. And with them, even more tourists.

The defense industry will continue to be strong, and even expand as companies seize an opportunity to rebuild destroyed facilities anew. Already, two additional shipbuilding operations — United States Marine and Trinity Yachts — have set up operations in South Mississippi.

Sounds and signs of progress are everywhere as major industries return to production at levels higher than ever. Car dealerships, despite trucking in used cars from all over the country, cannot keep up with the demand for replacement vehicles. Hospitals have shut down tent operations at their front doors after reopening floors as they are repaired and cleaned.

U.S. 90, the major beach highway, is all but repaired. Popular beachside restaurants like Long Beach Lookout, now U.S. 49 Lookout, have relocated inland. Schools have reopened in hastily patched buildings, temporary trailers or with double-session days.

And residents, determined to get back to their old ways, held the annual Peter Anderson Festival, which draws more than 100,000 yearly to Ocean Springs. In Bay St. Louis, Second Saturday, a sidewalk gathering of artists, vendors and restaurants, has returned. Walter Anderson Museum became the first Coast museum to reopen.

Scores of designers, planners, artists, architects, code specialists and others have completed a whirlwind of forum meetings intended to give the public tools and a new vision for their cities. Design plans are being released for 11 communities that fuse retail, living and green spaces. The goal: Balance vision and history.

"If we do our job well, then what is going to happen is Mississippi will be the standard-bearer and the example to the whole nation of how to build things well," said Steve Mouzon, a Miami-based architect who is leading the Mississippi Renewal Forum's architectural team.

As Jim Barksdale, head of the Governor's Commission on Recovery, Rebuilding and Renewal, put it, "Out of this terrible tragedy comes a great opportunity."

"It's the worst of times, but the best of times to plan," Barksdale said. "We've got the cleanest slate we're ever going to have, and the most attention from people who count, people around the world, that we'll ever have. We're looking at the greatest infusion of resources in an area that's not a war zone in history.

"This will be the greatest rebuilding project in the history of the world."

INDUSTRIAL MIGHT

As early as colonial times, shipbuilding was an important coastal industry. Location is one reason; the availability of construction wood, the other. Wars, including WWI, brought more shipbuilding. And then in 1938 came the granddaddy of them all, Ingalls Shipyard Corp. in Pascagoula. In 1997 the shipyard, one of the region's biggest industrial engines, became part of Northrop Grumman and now employs some 12,000 workers. Other major employers include Keesler Air Force Base (16,259); Grand Casino (4,900); Naval Construction Battalion Center (4,741); Stennis Space Center (4,531); Beau Rivage casino (2,459); Singing River Hospital (2,450); Memorial Hospital (2,336); Naval Station Pascagoula (2,205); and Harrison County Schools (1,706). JOHN C. FITZHUGH

FISHING A WAY OF LIFE

Is it the memorable sunsets or the many possibilities of fish that first drew settlers to Mississippi shores? One is good for the visual soul, the other for sustenance, be it casting a net for mullet in the sound and bays or dropping a bamboo pole line in a bayou. Through changing times, water, sunsets and fishing paint a coastal palette.

TIM ISBELL

Festivals galore

Bruce Davis of Gulfport throws a pot during the Ocean Springs Peter Anderson Festival, which draws more than 100,000 visitors. The numerous festivals, including the biggest festival of all - Mardi Gras - help define the culture of the Mississippi Coast. Besides the visual arts, festivals also help acknowledge a vibrant performing arts community that includes talented musical and theatrical performers. JOHN C. FITZHUGH

PINEYWOOD CANOPIES

The Mississippi Coast is a sea of green as well as blue. The forests, mostly pine, catered to Native Americans, then to the lumberman's ax. The felling of ancient yellow pine forests brought life to such cities as Gulfport and Pascagoula for exporting. In more recent times, the pineywoods claim a mixed use, from hunting and secluded living to recreation for trekkers, such as trails in DeSoto National Forest, and to lumber and paper company harvesting. JOHN C. FITZHUGH

LIFE UNDER THE OAKS

Pat Mowry's Win Rush house sat under an oak tree on Scenic Drive in Pass Christian. Visitors and residents driving along U.S. 90 from Pascagoula to Bay St. Louis could enjoy the historic and beautiful homes. The annual Spring Pilgrimage and several home tours featured the stately mansions that prominently lined the Coast highway overlooking the Mississippi Sound.
TIM ISBELL

CITIES WITH A VIEW

A couple walks down the Vieux Marché in downtown Biloxi on a relaxing day. Downtown areas in many of the cities along the Coast have become historic districts that serve as cultural centers and provide a mercantile niche to compete with larger retail outlets.
DAVID PURDY

BEACH LIFE

Welcomed public beach access distinguishes the Mississippi Coast from resorts that allow waterfront developments to hide views and waterways. Numerous municipal fishing piers, as good for a stroll as for wetting a hook, miles of groomed sand, rentals of beach water toys and inviting secluded sections with sand dunes, these and more define a coastline regularly replenished with sand when erosion takes its natural toll. DAVID PURDY

CALL OF THE WATER

"Shrimp boats a'comin!" Beginning with wooden sailing schooners in the late 1800s to the motorized steel-haul trawlers of modern time, the Coast's bounty of shrimp and oysters have required a working fleet. At rest in harbors from Bayou Caddy in Hancock County to Pass Christian, even Biloxi's Back Bay, the fleets are postcard pretty.
TIM ISBELL

Two days before Katrina made up her mind about where to go, South Mississippians faced decisions that would affect their lives forever. Many didn't evacuate, thinking, "My house made it through Camille." Others thought the storm would steer more toward Louisiana, sparing the Coast the worst. Evacuation orders went out at dawn the day before and the mad scramble began to fill up cars, move valuables to higher ground, purchase generators and dry goods and find reliable transportation or shelter.

A FRIGHT TO BEHOLD

An infrared satellite image from the National Oceanic and Atmospheric Administration shows the outer bands of Hurricane Katrina, well ashore on the Gulf Coast and the eye about 165 miles south-southeast of New Orleans at 8:15 p.m. CDT Sunday, Aug. 28, 2005. South Mississippi braced for 180 mph winds and a 25-foot storm surge. Forecasters warned that the storm could be as catastrophic, or more so, than Hurricane Camille, which had been the most powerful storm to hit land in U.S. history.
ASSOCIATED PRESS/NOAA

THIS IS BIG

Harrison County Emergency Management Agency Director Joe Spraggins and Harrison County leaders grapple with how to handle the gigantic storm approaching Mississippi and Louisiana.
DAVID PURDY

WE HAD A PLAN

Gulfport Fire Chief Pat Sullivan discusses his concerns about heavy rain and flooding in low-lying areas in Harrison County during a meeting with the Harrison County Emergency Management Agency and Harrison County leaders the day before the storm. DAVID PURDY

Got any gas?

Edgewater Mall maintenance employee Steve Buckley fills up with premium gas on Pass Road in Biloxi. The Shell station was out of regular unleaded fuel for 4½ hours because of the high demand before the storm hit. The bag-covered pumps were a sign of times to come when gas stations from South Mississippi to Arkansas ran dry for the lines of customers hoping to fill generators and cars. David Purdy

THRILL IS GONE

All 13 Gulf Coast casinos closed by 2 a.m. Sunday, Aug. 28, 2005. Guests were emptied out of hotels and slot machines counted as the storm approached. DREW TARTER

WHICH WAY OUT?

Master Sgt. Layne Girouard of Biloxi (left) and Sgt. Michael Clayton of Gulfport offer directions to motorists in Picayune after the two-state contraflow traffic plan closed southbound I-59 in Pearl River County. The two Mississippi Department of Transportation officers were part of the team helping to evacuate Louisiana residents. Contraflow allows Louisiana residents access to more highway lanes to evacuate. But drivers from both states inched along in bumper-to-bumper traffic, traveling only 45 miles in about four hours. JOHN C. FITZHUGH

SCHOOL SHELTER

Children sleep in the hallway at the Red Cross shelter at Vancleave High School. Nearly 600 people took refuge at the school.   DREW TARTER

BOATS LEAVING

Shrimp boats and pleasure craft leave the Biloxi Small Craft Harbor in Biloxi on the Saturday before Hurricane Katrina struck the Gulf Coast. JOHN C. FITZHUGH

SEEKING HIGHER GROUND

An employee of McElroy's Seafood Restaurant in Biloxi, a gulfside favorite for locals, rides a trailer-load of chairs and other furnishings removed from the restaurant. Most of the restaurants along the shore and beach highway would be destroyed. DREW TARTER

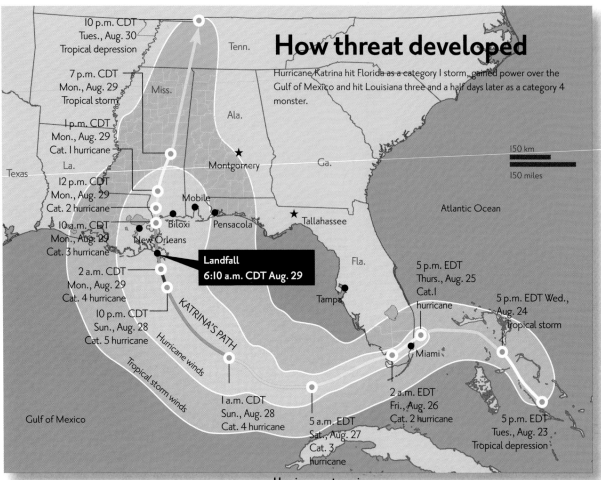

How threat developed

Hurricane Katrina hit Florida as a category I storm, gained power over the Gulf of Mexico and hit Louisiana three and a half days later as a category 4 monster.

10 p.m. CDT
Tues., Aug. 30
Tropical depression

7 p.m. CDT
Mon., Aug. 29
Tropical storm

1 p.m. CDT
Mon., Aug. 29
Cat. I hurricane

12 p.m. CDT
Mon., Aug. 29
Cat. 2 hurricane

10 a.m. CDT
Mon., Aug. 29
Cat. 3 hurricane

2 a.m. CDT
Mon., Aug. 29
Cat. 4 hurricane

10 p.m. CDT
Sun., Aug. 28
Cat. 5 hurricane

1 a.m. CDT
Sun., Aug. 28
Cat. 4 hurricane

5 a.m. EDT
Sat., Aug. 27
Cat. 3 hurricane

2 a.m. EDT
Fri., Aug. 26
Cat. 2 hurricane

5 p.m. EDT
Thurs., Aug. 25
Cat.I hurricane

5 p.m. EDT Wed.,
Aug. 24
Tropical storm

5 p.m. EDT
Tues., Aug. 23
Tropical depression

Landfall
6:10 a.m. CDT Aug. 29

KATRINA'S PATH

Hurricane winds

Tropical storm winds

Tenn.

Miss.

Ala.

La.

Texas

Montgomery

Mobile

Biloxi

Pensacola

New Orleans

Tallahassee

Ga.

Fla.

Tampa

Miami

Atlantic Ocean

Gulf of Mexico

150 km

150 miles

WEATHER CHANNEL COVERAGE

Jim Cantore, a meteorologist for the Weather Channel, does a live broadcast from Biloxi Beach on the Saturday before Katrina struck the Gulf Coast. JOHN C. FITZHUGH

Hurricane categories

	Tropical storm	Category I	Category 2	Category 3	Category 4	Category 5
Wind speed	39-74 mph (63-119 kph)	74-95 mph (119-153 kph)	96-110 mph (154-177 kph)	111-130 mph (178-209 kph)	131-155 mph (210-249 kph)	155+ mph (250+ kph)
Storm surge	Less than 5 ft. (1.5 m)	4-5 ft. (1.2-1.5 m)	6-8 ft. (1.8-2.4 m)	9-12 ft. (2.7-3.7 m)	13-18 ft. (4-5.5 m)	More than 18 ft. (5.5 m)

Source: National Hurricane Center   Graphic: Helen Lee McComas, Lee Hulteng, Pai

© 2005 KRT

ALL ROADS LEAD OUT

Evacuees travel east on U.S. Highway 90 in Pascagoula away from Katrina on Sunday. One survey of evacuees showed that as many as 30 percent possibly would not return to South Mississippi. JOHN C. FITZHUGH

CHAPTER 2

CHAOS & TEARS

HARD KNOCKED

Benjamin Rowe of Biloxi wanted to buy charcoal at the Kmart at Cowan and Pass roads but despaired after he was told the store had none. Although it had no power, the store opened on a cash-only basis to sell necessities. DREW TARTER

SEARCHING FOR THE DEAD

Firefighters Brian Goecke (from right) Ronald Floyd and Bud Lindsey, look for the bodies of a Long Beach couple but discovered they had been found by another team. Teams continued to search for missing people months after the storm struck. JOHN C. FITZHUGH

'YOUR CITY IS GONE'

By Anita Lee

Hurricane Katrina's winds stopped the clocks in downtown Biloxi at 6:05 a.m., Aug. 29, 2005.

From Pascagoula to Waveland, residents hunkered down for a Camille-like storm. The sound of the wind was a cross between a shriek and whistle as it tore through trees and buildings.

From their homes, residents watched trees bend and snap, and tin peel from roofs like skin off an apple. This, they thought, would be the worst of it.

Later, the National Weather Service listed Katrina as a Category 3 storm with maximum sustained winds in South Mississippi of 125 mph.

This was no Camille. A Category 5, Camille clocked in at 200 mph and higher.

But then came the water. It slammed ashore and surged inland. Nothing compared to this. The old flood measurements from Camille were out the window.

Katrina left her mark as the worst natural disaster in American history.

From the second floor of city hall, Biloxi Mayor A.J. Holloway watched in horror. "This," he said, "is our tsunami."

In Jackson and Hancock counties, emergency operation crews were forced to abandon their buildings. Pass Christian police officers swam for their lives.

In Bay St. Louis, Beach Boulevard resident Kelvin Schulz asked himself, "What have I gotten my family into?" From a second-floor apartment, he urged his children onto the roof. His 80-year-old mother-in-law, Jane Mollere, refused to budge.

"Kelvin," she said, "I'm too old for this."

And so she drowned, as did dozens of others.

The statewide fatality count from Hurricane Katrina stands at more than 225, with more than 175 of those in the six Coast counties.

A larger number of residents clung to life in treetops, attics and boats, and on rooftops as seas of rubble swept past. Much of the Coast's treasured history, its antebellum homes and graceful public buildings, floated in that rubble.

Heroes abounded. Firefighters and other public employees plucked stranded residents from waterlogged perches as the wind continued to howl; sons, fathers, mothers or daughters urged other family members to safety.

Families who possessed lofty attics gathered neighbors and herded them up the stairs.

Many residents told of loved ones who called to say they were trapped just before the phone went dead. The lucky ones were reunited after hours, or even days, of worry.

The National Weather Service set Katrina's landfall, when the eye comes ashore, at 6:10 a.m. Aug. 29, 2005, in Plaquemines Parish, La., and a second time at 10 a.m. on the Mississippi-Louisiana line.

The wind was still howling, although the water had subsided, when a newspaper photographer left the building on the Gulfport-Biloxi line, just north of the CSX railroad tracks, at 1:15 p.m. He drove a few miles into Gulfport and then Biloxi. Thirty minutes later he returned, beaten by the wind.

Because he was from Tallahassee, Fla., and the damage was so great, the photographer did not realize he had been to two different localities. No matter, his words could have applied to any of the distinct waterfront communities from Waveland to Biloxi's eastern tip.

The photographer said to those of us seated in the groaning building, "Your city is gone."

NEIGHBORHOOD CHECK

Pete Mestas wades in chest-deep water after checking on elderly neighbors in Channel Mark subdivision in Biloxi as Hurricane Katrina whipped the Mississippi Gulf Coast.
MIKE YACKSYZN II

A MOTHER'S COMFORT

Beth Stump cradles her 9-week-old daughter, Breanna, as the two wait to get food from the Salvation Army in East Biloxi three days after Katrina. PATRICK SCHNEIDER

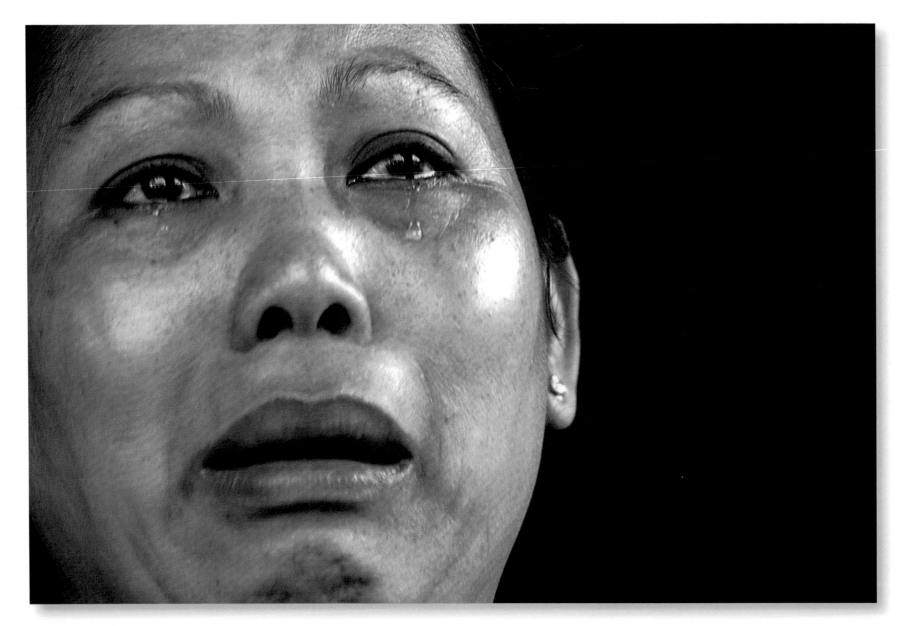

'Baby, don't die'

Kim Nguyen, 50, weeps as she describes how she clutched her 3-year-old son while crouching in the attic as water from Katrina encircled her ankles. "I said, 'Baby don't die. If you die, I die.'" They survived but the family's home, work places and belongings were destroyed, a fate suffered by hundreds in Vietnamese neighborhoods in Biloxi. She is a seamstress, but her shop was demolished. Nick Oza

Toughest job

Firefighters remove a body from an East Biloxi house the day after the hurricane. Of the more than 225 killed statewide by the storm, most lost their lives in Biloxi. PATRICK SCHNEIDER

BEATEN UP

Mangled vehicles lie amid piles of debris from homes and other buildings at Porter Avenue and Beach Boulevard in Biloxi. DREW TARTER

BOULEVARD OF DESTRUCTION

Beach Boulevard, the cultural and entertainment heart of downtown Bay St. Louis, was demolished by the 30-foot storm surge from Katrina.
DAVID PURDY

WATERLOGGED

Cars evacuated to the side of Mississippi 603 in Bay St. Louis before Katrina sit in a flooded ditch the day after the hurricane.

JOHN C. FITZHUGH

Steps to nowhere

Randy Wright of Biloxi takes a break on a set of steps on Howard Avenue as President George Bush visits the city. Wright, a city public works employee who lost his house on Claiborne Avenue, got to shake the president's hand. "I was glad to meet him. He seemed like he was sincere." John C. Fitzhugh

DISPLACED

After the winds and water subsided, residents woke up to find lots of things out of place. A car was tossed into a swimming pool, left, at what was once the Magnolia Condominiums on Beach Boulevard in Biloxi. Off Howard Avenue in Biloxi, bottom left, debris filled what used to be a neighborhood. In Bernard Bayou near Kremer Marine in Gulfport, bottom right, docked pleasure boats were washed ashore. DREW TARTER, TIM ISBELL

What's this...?

A common refrain on the Coast was, "What's this doing in my yard?" The surge from the hurricane caused several tractor trailers containing frozen chicken and other freight from the Mississippi State Port to float into west Gulfport neighborhoods. Tony Webb of Allendale Avenue, left, surrounded by debris pushed into his yard, rode out Katrina in his home with 4 feet of water inside. Webb said most items in his home were covered in mud and water and there was nothing worth saving. The frame of a Crowley truck, bottom, was wrapped around an oak tree on U.S. 90 in Gulfport. David Purdy, John C. Fitzhugh

Ravaged

The Isle of Capri Casino and Resort on U.S. 90 in Biloxi suffered heavy damage as did all of the Coast's casinos along the beach highway. DAVID PURDY

ROADS GONE

Ocean Springs residents, above, make their way through debris on Washington Avenue. The Ocean Springs U.S. 90 bridge, right, a major connector between Harrison and Jackson counties, was devastated by high winds and the flood surge. DREW TARTER, DAVID PURDY

Signs of the time

A spray-painted sign marks the address of a home on Beach Boulevard in Pascagoula. Nearly all of the picturesque homes along this beachfront street in Pascagoula were destroyed by the wind and storm surge. DAVID PURDY

Point Cadet area ripped

A day after Katrina, the Casino Magic Biloxi barge rests on the north side of U.S. 90 in Biloxi, next to the St. Michael's Catholic Church by the Sea. Point Cadet, an area rich in heritage, once was woods, with great hunting and fishing, when the seafood factories came in the late 1800s. Immigrant families became the backbone of The Point – first the Slavonians, then the Louisiana French and much later the Vietnamese – all lured to shuck oysters, peel shrimp or work the boats. David Purdy

NEIGHBORHOOD LOST

Barb Sciulli (left) walks down Coleman Avenue in Waveland with her nephews, Nathan and Hayden Kren of Bay St. Louis. This was one of several Waveland neighborhoods obliterated by Katrina. JOHN C. FITZHUGH

SURVIVAL MODE

In the immediate days after Katrina, survivors found shelter under tents and tarps, placed even atop the ruins of their lost homes. These Back Bay residents rest after salvaging what they could find in the remains of their Biloxi home. BRANDI JADE THOMAS

HIGH AND DRY

Pleasure craft from the Ocean Springs Small Craft Harbor, left, washed onto shore with other debris caught in Katrina's surge. The shrimp boat "Knowledge," above, rested on the shore along the Industrial Seaway in Gulfport. DAVID PURDY, MIKE CARDEW

Hard times

The conditions at the Oakwood Villa apartments were hard to take for young and old. Most of the residents had to flee to the second floor of the apartments to escape the storm surge. Their homes were a muddy mess and their belongings lined the walkways. The apartments are near a water treatment plant, and many residents feared that sewage entered their homes with Katrina's wave. TIM ISBELL

Oh, what a relief

Gulfport neighbors (from left) August Parker, William Manning and Nora and Leo Necaise find relief from the heat and humidity as they use a makeshift shower. They tapped into a city water pipe to take their first shower since the hurricane. BRIAN BLANCO

OUTDOOR ROOM

Gary Stilwell (left) and Nicholas Lacour sit on the foundation of Stilwell's home in East Biloxi. Stilwell rode out the storm in his two-story house until the flood surge washed it away, forcing him and his wife to swim to his boat. Once on the boat, Stilwell rescued five women during the raging storm. In the aftermath, the lack of electricity and safe buildings forced most residents outside to eat and cook. TIM ISBELL

STACK OF RUBBLE

A child's doll rests on a pile of rubble in the Point Cadet area of Biloxi. The toy seems to have made it through the storm intact, unlike the house that held it. MIKE CARDEW

AT LEAST THERE'S GAS

Motorists wait in line to purchase fuel in Biloxi four days after Katrina destroyed or crippled most service stations in the area. Some motorists reported waiting in the line as long as four hours to travel just four miles to pumps where regular unleaded was selling at $4 a gallon. BRIAN BLANCO

SMASHED CARGO

An industrial transport barge lies amid other debris from cargo containers that burst open when they were washed from storage at the state port in Gulfport. DAVID PURDY

Water swept

An overstuffed reclining chair sits on the south shore of Deer Island. The island was littered with debris blown in by the wind or carried in by the storm's surge.
David Purdy

PROTECTING GAS AND GENERATORS

Danny Brewer shows he means business about the sign at the end of Tarpon Drive in Gautier. Brewer said the people at his house had been sleeping in shifts to keep an eye on their gas and generators. "It just scares me," he said. JOHN C. FITZHUGH

WRECKAGE ON THE BEACHES

Boat captain Robert L. Brodie of Biloxi walks along the south shore of Deer Island, which was strewn with wreckage of every description.
DAVID PURDY

ALL BETS OFF

Ruined slot machines and other debris from the Grand Casino in Biloxi cover the ground along U.S. 90. KARL MONDON

KATRINA'S MARCH

Katrina left much of U.S. 90, the beach highway, impassable. These were the westbound lanes in Long Beach. JOHN C. FITZHUGH

RAKED AND WHIPPED

The Ocean Springs Yacht Club (right) was washed away along with the U.S. 90
Ocean Springs bridge by the onslaught of wind and water. DAVID PURDY

STRANDED ON DOCK

Chau Nguyen sits in a temporary home he and his wife, Le, made for themselves along the Industrial Seaway in Gulfport. Le, who was five months' pregnant with twins, and her husband found shelter atop a dock two days after the hurricane made landfall. The dock was just 100 yards from their shrimp boat (in background on the right) and they were reluctant to leave the dock for fear of losing their possessions to looters. Chau said the fact that they stuck by each other means that he truly loves her and that she truly loves him. CHRIS STANFIELD

Found it!

Bill Fandison, 68, reacts as he finds an antique pull cart that he had been searching for in the rubble of what used to be his shop in a Waveland flea market. BRIAN BLANCO

ROAD NO MORE

The storm surge washed away large sections of Beach Boulevard, which took residents and tourists to downtown Bay St. Louis. DAVID PURDY

Damaged grandeur

Biloxi's Tivoli Hotel, built in 1927, was one of the few remaining Coast grand dame resorts from the 1920s. According to newspaper accounts, the Tivoli opened "in a whirl of dancing, a kaleidoscopic blaze of color and a musical festival of barbaric jazz." But then, Katrina came. While the Tivoli suffered major damage, the Biloxi Yacht Club, which sat between the hotel and U.S. 90 — where emergency workers are standing — was wiped away by the tidal surge. PATRICK SCHNEIDER

ARE WE THERE YET?

Demetrius Thomas, 2, of Biloxi sits in line at the Red Cross check distribution site at the United Artists Biloxi 10 Theater parking lot. Demetrius' house was flooded with 8 feet of water, said his father, Fred. The two had arrived at the site at 6 a.m. to get a spot in line with about 100 people in front of them. JOHN C. FITZHUGH

Giant sharkhead gone

A souvenir shop that used to sport a giant shark head as an entrance to the business at U.S. 90 and Rodenberg Avenue in Biloxi was reduced to rubble. David Purdy

No place to go

Mary H. Jackson was evicted from her home of four years on Briarfield Avenue in Biloxi after a domestic dispute she had with her boyfriend. Jackson said she had 30 days to find a new home, but new places to live are hard to find after the hurricane. Hundreds of others living in rental properties found themselves in similar emergencies when landlords began to repair and rebuild damaged units. Open apartment units and houses for sale were snapped up by displaced residents immediately after the storm. David Purdy

Storm survivor

The tugboat S.S. Hurricane Camille, which was washed ashore during Camille in 1969, has survived another major hurricane. There are two stories about the tugboat. One states that the tug was sunk in the Gulfport harbor near the location of the Copa Casino, and the surge of Camille moved it. The other says repair work was just completed on the tug, which was preparing to return to sea when the legendary storm hit. JOHN C. FITZHUGH

Hunting for victims

An Urban Search and Rescue team from the South Florida Task Force searches for bodies in a wrecked boat that was found washed ashore in Pass Christian. AL DIAZ

Nearly all of a condominium complex on St. Charles Street on U.S. 90 in Biloxi, along with a nearby neighborhood of homes, was wiped out. DAVID PURDY

WHAT A MESS

Bobbie Hawkins can't believe that cargo containers from the Mississippi state port in Gulfport ended up next to her home on Rich Avenue. Hawkins was salvaging what was left of her belongings. Hurricane debris, including rotting chicken in the container behind her, had kept Hawkins and her family from being able to enter the area safely. DAVID PURDY

Cynthia and Dan McEldowney apply for FEMA help after her home was destroyed. Long lines and weary faces were a common sight for weeks. AL DIAZ

Disease scare

Amid fears of a dysentery outbreak, nurses carry children to a health tent for examination after FEMA and police ordered the evacuation of the shelter at the Mary L. Michel Seventh Grade School in Biloxi. The shelter held hundreds of people but had no functional plumbing. The evacuees were loaded on buses and taken to a Red Cross shelter in Georgia. NICK OZA

OUT OF PLACE

A Pass Christian police cruiser rests on a tree after floating into the middle of this cemetery. Cemeteries across South Mississippi were damaged by Katrina's wind and water.
AL DIAZ

Treasure found

Antiques dealer Tom Waldon searched through the mud for depression glass and china where his home once stood along North Beach Boulevard in Bay Saint Louis. Here, Waldon holds a demitasse cup found in the rubble. Many paintings and antiques went the way of the wind and water in Bay St. Louis, known for its artists, small shops and beachside cafes. AL DIAZ

Sign language

Not far from steps leading to an empty slab where a home once stood, above, a piece of plywood bears a message from a resident on U.S. 90 in Gulfport. Throughout the area, residents displayed messages of hope, sadness, frustration, warnings and even humor. Humor wins out in the Open House/Sale Pending signs, right, sitting in the rubble in front of what had been a Waveland home. DAVID PURDY, TIM ISBELL

A RAVAGED ENVIRONMENT

Katrina's wind and waves took a significant toll on wildlife, fishing piers, waters and forests. Millions of trees were downed within a few hours, affecting animals' habitat and rearranging forests. Chemicals, sewage and debris contaminated and clogged bays and bayous. The Biloxi Small Craft Harbor, top photo, will have to be redesigned and restored. Behind the Isle of Capri Casino, a large plastic bag of salad dressing floating in the water catches the casino's reflection. This sea otter, right, was spotted in east Pass Christian at the pier across from Wal-Mart. It probably was blown in from the barrier islands during the storm.

DAVID PURDY, JOHN C. FITZHUGH

MUD SLINGING

Andrew and Matt Barrett try to dig out their 1969 Coronet from the dried mud in Pass Christian. They had moved it to higher ground for safekeeping. AL DIAZ

THANKFUL WORSHIP

James Byrd of Biloxi joins fellow parishioners in giving thanks to God during a worship service the first Sunday after Katrina at the Episcopal Church of the Redeemer in Biloxi. The service was held outside under the few remaining oaks. TIM ISBELL, NICK OZA

ANSWERED PRAYERS

On the first Sunday after the hurricane, people recalled their prayers during the harrowing hours of Katrina. Nan Lovett, embraced by Elizabeth Foley at St. Mark's Episcopal Church on U.S. 90 in Gulfport, said she took refuge in her attic a block from the beach as the surge rose. "All we did was pray my daughter would come and rescue us. And at 5 o'clock, she came." NICK OZA

No access

Sgt. Paul Kushma of the 116th Infantry in Charlottesville, Va., stands guard at the 33rd Avenue railroad crossing in Gulfport. Access to the areas south of the railroad tracks, which suffered the most destruction from Katrina, were limited for health and safety reasons. Residents had to wait to gain access to their properties.
John C. Fitzhugh

TRUTH SURVIVES

A message for survivors on a bench on Pass Road in Biloxi.
JOHN C. FITZHUGH

DISPLACED

Terry Musgrove of the Village Apartments in Gulfport shows his medical ID medallion. He was just one of many special-needs residents who were bused off the Gulf Coast and relocated north of Jackson, Miss., because their apartments were heavily damaged. DAVID PURDY

Overturned

Mounted Orlando, Fla., policemen Jeff Angel and Michael Garcia ride past a vintage Corvette as they patrol in Pass Christian. AL DIAZ

STREETS OF RUIN

Debris fill what used to be a neighborhood off of Howard Avenue in Biloxi. Most of the wooden structures and homes on Point Cadet were demolished by the combination of high winds and a 30-foot tidal surge. TIM ISBELL

TREASURE BAY AGROUND

The Treasure Bay Casino was washed from its moorings onto shore in Biloxi. The casino had been battered by previous storms, but Katrina destroyed the Coast landmark. DREW TARTER

Battered beachfront

The Belle Fontaine Beach area of Jackson County near the city of Ocean Springs was destroyed by high winds and the flood surge. Nothing was left but concrete slabs where beachfront homes used to stand. David Purdy

BEFORE AND AFTER

HISTORY LOST

This 1900s Queen Anne house was renovated in 1999 to become the Chimneys, a fine-dining restaurant owned by Peter and Dix Nord, who moved from the Long Beach Harbor site to the house on Gulfport's Beach Boulevard. The work the Nords put into the house was cited in 2004 by the Gulfport Downtown Association as a significant contribution to revitalizing the area. After Katrina, facing page, it was a heap of rubble. Tammy Smith

END OF AN ERA

Biloxi Beach Park on U.S. 90 in Biloxi was an attraction for Coast residents and tourists for decades. Hurricane Katrina obliterated the popular amusement park, facing page. JOHN C. FITZHUGH

REARRANGEMENT

The Isle of Capri and Casino Magic, in the heart of Biloxi's Casino Row, are seen in these photos taken before and after Katrina struck from Grand Casino's parking garage at Pine Street and U.S. 90. The Casino Magic gaming barge, facing page, was washed across the highway and into a parking lot. JOHN C. FITZHUGH

High Water Marks

HARRISON COUNTY

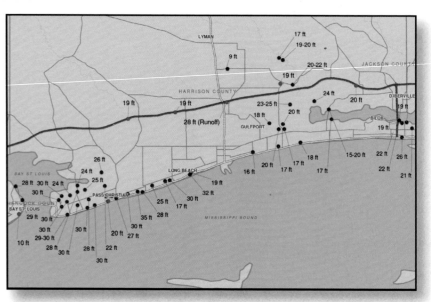

HANCOCK COUNTY

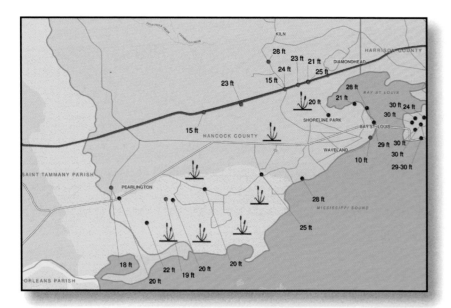

- ● FEMA High Water Marks
- ● USGS High Water Marks

JACKSON COUNTY

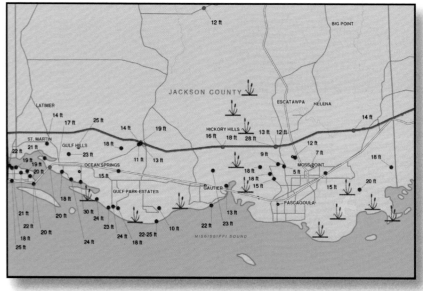

Katrina's surge

The storm surge from Hurricane Katrina inundated South Mississippi's coastline.

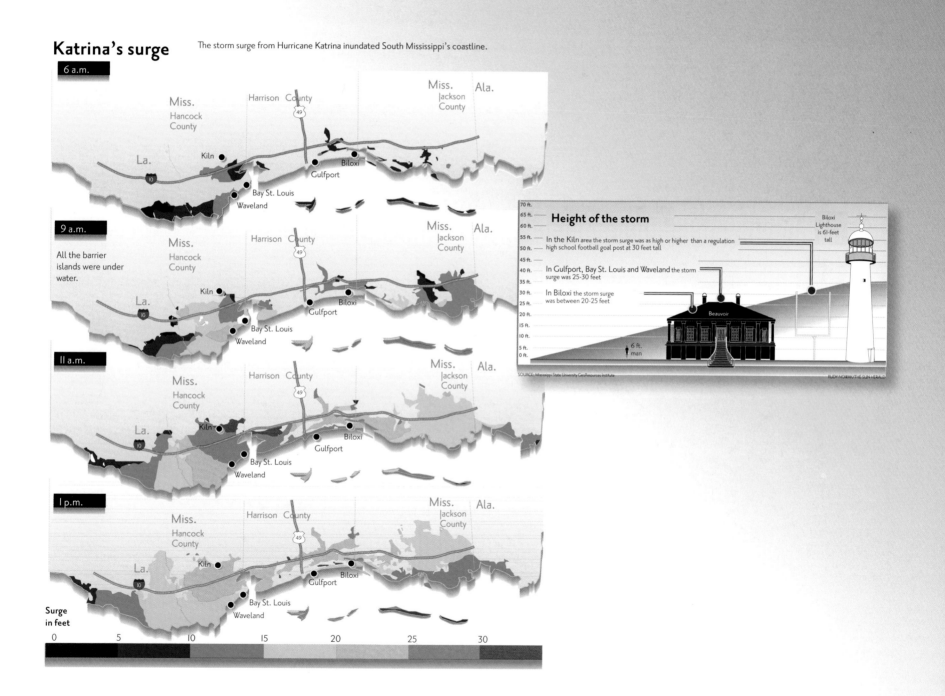

6 a.m.

Miss.
Hancock County

Harrison County

Miss.
Jackson County

Ala.

La.

Kiln

Biloxi
Gulfport

Bay St. Louis
Waveland

9 a.m.

All the barrier islands were under water.

Miss.
Hancock County

Harrison County

Miss.
Jackson County

Ala.

La.

Kiln

Biloxi
Gulfport

Bay St. Louis
Waveland

11 a.m.

Miss.
Hancock County

Harrison County

Miss.
Jackson County

Ala.

La.

Kiln

Biloxi
Gulfport

Bay St. Louis
Waveland

1 p.m.

Miss.
Hancock County

Harrison County

Miss.
Jackson County

Ala.

La.

Kiln

Biloxi
Gulfport

Bay St. Louis
Waveland

Surge in feet

0   5   10   15   20   25   30

Height of the storm

70 ft.
65 ft.
60 ft.
55 ft.
50 ft.
45 ft.
40 ft.
35 ft.
30 ft.
25 ft.
20 ft.
15 ft.
10 ft.
5 ft.
0 ft.

In the Kiln area the storm surge was as high or higher than a regulation high school football goal post at 30 feet tall

In Gulfport, Bay St. Louis and Waveland the storm surge was 25-30 feet

In Biloxi the storm surge was between 20-25 feet

Beauvoir

6 ft. man

Biloxi Lighthouse is 61-feet tall

SOURCE: Mississippi State University GeoResources Institute

RUDY NOWAK/THE SUN HERALD

We remember

MORE THAN 225 LIVES WERE TAKEN BY KATRINA

Katrina's death toll was still rising in November, more than two months after the storm. In Mississippi more than 225 lives were lost, including more than 175 in the six coastal counties of Hancock, Harrison, Jackson, Stone, Pearl River and George. Here are the names of the deceased that have been released. Information was gathered from coroners, family members, obituaries, newspaper stories and computer databases.

FOUR DEAD

Doug deSilvey of Biloxi was the only survivor after a wall of water swept away a house on Point Porteaux in the Gulf Hills area of St. Martin. Afterward, DeSilvey and other relatives posted crosses at what was left in honor of his ex-wife, Linda deSilvey, her parents, Nadine Allen-Gifford and Ted Gifford, and his daughter, Donna deSilvey. JOHN C. FITZHUGH

BARNEY ANDERSON, 83, GULFPORT
MARK ANDERSON, 52, BILOXI
SHEILA AULTMAN, 46, LONG BEACH
BETTY JUNE DEHART BAGLEY, 71, GULFPORT
ANNA REBECCA BALL
EDGAR BANE JR., 15, WAVELAND
EDGAR BANE SR., 48, WAVELAND
CARL BANE, 13, WAVELAND
CHRISTINA BANE, 45, WAVELAND
BERNT BASTIANSEN
KIM E. BELL, 51, BAY ST. LOUIS
STEPFORNO D. BELL, 21, BAY ST. LOUIS
GLORIA BENIGNO, 77, BAY ST. LOUIS
LUKEY BENIGNO, 82, BAY ST. LOUIS
NORMA BIELLER
LANDO BISHOP, 75, BILOXI
MALCOLM BLACKWOOD, MID-50S, PASCAGOULA
MYRA D. BOOKER, 42, BILOXI
LEE ESTHER BRANTLEY, 77, ST. MARTIN
MARGERY M. BRECHT, 82, BILOXI
JAMES LACEY BROWN, BILOXI
JOSEPH BROWN, 70, BILOXI
LINDA GERALDINE BROWN, 59, LONG BEACH
JOSEPH BRUGGER, 65, PASS CHRISTIAN
GEORGE L. BUCKLAND, 73, BILOXI
BILLIE CAIMI, 68, WAVELAND
JOSEPH CAMPBELL
PATRICIA CAREY, WAVELAND
JUDY COLLINS
WILLIAMS COLLINS
PATRICK CONWAY, 49, BILOXI
JOAN DAGNALL
RALPH DAGNALL

LEVEN DAWSON, 64, WAVELAND
ROSE DECORTE, 73, PASS CHRISTIAN
DONNA K. DESILVEY, 35, BILOXI
LINDA ALLEN DESILVEY, 57, BILOXI
JOHN DICKEY, 61, BILOXI
DONALD DOHERTY, 81, PASS CHRISTIAN
THOMAS DUNN, 90, BILOXI
DONALD DUPRE
MARY DYER
ALBERT FAGOT, 85, PEARLINGTON
MARION FAVRE, 83, WAVELAND
ANNA FRANKLIN, 75, BILOXI
CHARLES FRANKLIN, 84, BILOXI
PEARL FRAZIER, 96, BILOXI
CONNIE FRYMYRE
EUGENE GARCIA, 72, BAY ST. LOUIS
WILLIAM GARCIA
PATRICIA GEORGE, BAY ST. LOUIS
JERRY GIST
EDWARD W. "TED" GIFFORD, 79, OCEAN SPRINGS
NADINE L. ALLEN GIFFORD, 80, OCEAN SPRINGS
JERRY GIST
DANNY GOFF, 50, BILOXI
DENNIS GOVER
FAYE ROBERIE GRYCO, 70, BAY ST. LOUIS
BEVERLY GUNNELLS, 61, BILOXI
MICHAEL HARRISON
MICHAEL HARRIS
ULYSSES HEGLER, GULFPORT
DIETER HEIN, 71, DIAMONDHEAD
ROSIE HEIN, DIAMONDHEAD
BRYAN HICKMAN
CHIEKO HILBER, 75, PASS CHRISTIAN
LEROY HILBER, 64, PASS CHRISTIAN
JIM HILL
MARIE HILLARD, 70, BILOXI
JOHN HOLLEY, 68, BILOXI
OCTAVIA PAYTON HORNE, 78, BILOXI

Al-Amin Hunafa

Alonzo Husley, Woolmarket

Arthur W. Hyatt, 76, Pass Christian

Jean Hyatt, 74, Pass Christian

James Hyre, 83, Ocean Springs

Shamsi Hyre, 75, Ocean Springs

Evangelina Kamuf, 79, Waveland

Betty Kerr, 75, Pass Christian

Charles Kerr, 79, Pass Christian

Marie Knoblock, 63

Penny Krause

Norman Kreihn, 89, Biloxi

Nelson Lang

Helen Lang, 72, Pass Christian

Nelson Lang, 76, Pass Christian

Kenneth Lantier

Debra Ann Law, 49, Gulfport

Betty Lefler, Diamondhead

Janet Lynn, 92, Ocean Springs

James Madison

Ralph Madison

Charles Marsden, 81, Pass Christian

Ruth Marsden, Pass Christian

Gerald Marshall, 64, Gulfport

Marjorie Matrange

Roger Mattox

Harneitha Maxey, 75, Long Beach

Louis Maxey, 92, Long Beach

Timothy McCree

Debbie McKay

Patricia Meeks, 60, Waveland

Arthur Meunier III, 63, Pass Christian

Arthur Meunier

Scotty Michael

Sidney Miller, 79, Bay St. Louis

Linda Mims, 39, Biloxi

Jane Mollere, 80, Bay St. Louis

Linda Marie Moore, 45, Biloxi

Victoria Moore, 84, Biloxi

Wilfred Morgan

|William Morris, Pass Christian

James Moultrie, 53, Biloxi

Doris Murphy, 76, Waveland

Nancy Murphy, 86, Bay St. Louis

Horace Necaise Jr., 78, Pass Christian

Steven Nesossis, 34, Gulfport

John Noucher, 74, Long Beach

Joe Ben Parker, 65, Biloxi

James Patton, 22, Biloxi

Beverly Payne, 74, Gulfport

Paul Phillips, 91, Gulfport

James Pierce

Jack Prather, 65, Biloxi

Larry Preston, 61, Gulfport

Margaret Preston, 38, Gulfport

Scott Allen Preston, 34, Gulfport

James Silar Rainey II, 64, Biloxi

Kemp Ramsey, 54, Biloxi

Leroy Robinson, 55, Biloxi

Ione Mercedes Abbley Russell, 91, Pass Christian

Larry Russell, 67, Bay St. Louis

James Sanders

Lawrence Sanders, 57, Pearlington

Michael Santa Cruz, 47, Biloxi

Odessa Saucier, 90, Biloxi

William Leonard Schraberg, 61, Pass Christian

Van Alan Schultz, 69, Bay St. Louis

Allie Scott, 95, Waveland

Joseph Scott, 77, Waveland

Emma Anita Seals, 81, Pass Christian

Davis Hall Smith, 60, Waveland

Janice DeCorte Smith, 40, Pass Christian

Leon Ray Smith, 52, Gulfport

Richard Sherman Smith, 53, Biloxi

Anna Marie Storment, 41, Biloxi

John Matthew Tart, 2, Pass Christian

Samuel Francis Tart, 51, Pass Christian

James Taylor, 54, Biloxi

Standley Thomas, 51, Biloxi

Norma Jean (Parker) Trimmer, 66, Pass Christian

Guy Valvano

Collette Vierling, 51, Waveland

Gerald Raymond Vierling, 45, Waveland

Tony Vyehara

Rose Marie Walls, 56, Gulfport

Roland Watts

Henry L. Wescovich, 86, Biloxi

Brenda Ann Yetter, Long Beach

Valerie T. Zrinsky, 87, Ocean Springs

SWEPT AWAY

Emily Schulz sat on the rubble of the Star Theater in Bay St. Louis, where she last saw her mother, Jane Mollere, 80 (in photograph). Mollere decided to stay in the second floor of the building, saying it was time for her to die, while Schulz and the rest of her family escaped from a second-story window into the raging waters of Katrina's storm surge. Schulz' remains were found about a block away. CHRIS OCHSNER

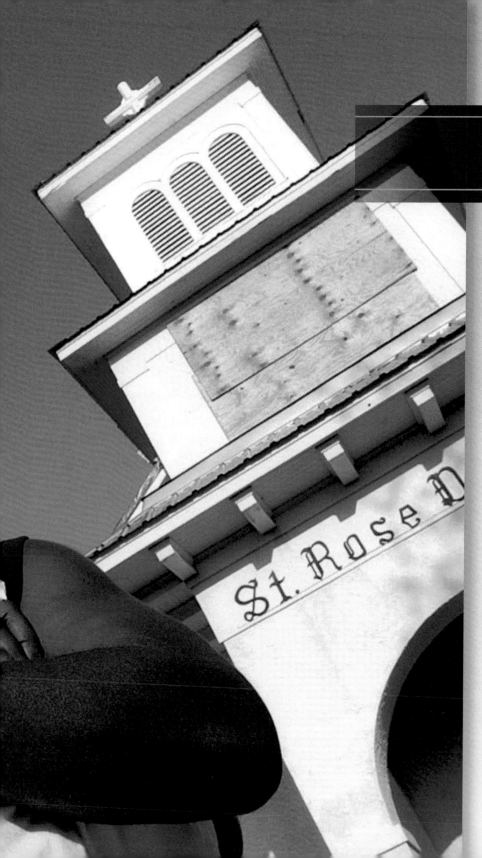

One mind, one heart

By Jim Mashek

Once the water from Hurricane Katrina receded, the helping hands appeared. Utility workers started restoring power, sewer and water service. Field hospitals were set up along the Coast. And volunteers from distant spots on the map showed up in droves.

Lanny Freeman was watching Katrina coverage on CNN in Tarpon Springs, Fla., when he decided he had to do something. He bought about $200 worth of supplies in the Florida Panhandle on his way to Hancock County. "I figured I had the time, I had the money, I might as well come up here," he said.

Freeman was part of a cast of thousands.

Alberto Cruz of Staten Island, N.Y., signed up for the Goodness Project, a faith-based initiative that set up shop in D'Iberville and brought relief to hundreds of families left homeless by the storm. "What does this mean to me?" Cruz asked. "I'm doing God's work. It's spiritual."

Churches were fundamental to the recovery. The Rev. Louis Lohan, pastor of St. Thomas Catholic Church in Long Beach, held Mass for a while at Quarles Elementary School. The entire St. Thomas complex had been destroyed.

"I think the church has started the healing process," Lohan said. "Anytime you can get people together, you put the recovery in motion."

Beth Faul, with her infant daughter in hand, helped prepare hot meals for all comers at the Bay Vista Baptist Church.

A special Sabbath

Sam Dorsey hugs friend and neighbor Holly Hayden in front of the storm-damaged and powerless St. Rose de Lima Catholic Church in Bay St. Louis on the Sunday after Katrina. Brian Blanco

WATER BOTTLES OF RELIEF

Judy Styron of Biloxi carries water and ice she picked up at a FEMA distribution center in the parking lot of the Biloxi Wal-Mart. JOHN C. FITZHUGH

"Last Sunday, before the storm even hit, we got together and decided that was what we were going to do," she said.

Residents and public officials from San Bernardino County, Calif., helped raise about $500,000 in money, gift cards and supplies for Gulfport.

"It's overwhelming, and unreal," Gulfport mayor Brent Warr said.

Not really, in the mind of Paul Leon, the mayor of Ontario, Calif.

"This, to me, is being American."

SORTING FOR SIZES

Winona Knott of the Woolmarket community outside Biloxi looks for clothes for her great-grandchildren at a relief distribution point in Biloxi. As she searched, her granddaughter waited in line for gas. Katrina destroyed her granddaughter's home in Ocean Springs.
JOHN C. FITZHUGH

PRESIDENTIAL SYMPATHY

President George Bush comforts Kim Bassier (left) and Bronwynne Bassier as he tours Howard Avenue in Biloxi four days after the storm. Bronwynne broke down in tears as she told the president she lost everything but the clothes she was wearing. TIM ISBELL

HELPING HER HOMETOWN

Mississippi Gulf Coast native Robin Roberts, an ABC "Good Morning America" anchor, helps Home Depot volunteers from Destin, Fla., unload a supply trailer in a warehouse near Pass Christian High School. Roberts, along with "Good Morning America" Gets It Done, Americorps, Home Depot, Staples and Salvation Army volunteers, brought supplies and labor to Pass Christian to help residents. DAVID PURDY

We've got power

Utility crews from around the country descended on the Gulf Coast to help restore power to hundreds of thousands of residents. The quick restoration of power to most areas was one of the first success stories of the relief effort. JOHN C. FITZHUGH

Bags for the needy

Joe Washington of Gulfport carries a bag of supplies he received at a relief center. Supplies were slow in arriving to the Coast the first week after the storm. John C. Fitzhugh

In ruins

Ayana Russell, 14, walks through the insulation that covered the floor of the Grace Temple Baptist Church in Gulfport as she explores the damage. John C. Fitzhugh

Food brings a smile

Thomas Arguell, 10, smiles as he walks away with MREs (Meals, Ready to Eat) he got for his family. The National Guard provided thousands of the prepackaged meals for survivors standing in line for food and water at a relief center at the Crossroads Mall in Gulfport. Nick Oza

Red Cross to the rescue

Tra Van Nguyen (center, bottom photograph) talks with Red Cross volunteers Loretta Ehrler (left) and Dr. Thomas Conran at his home on Bayview Drive in Pass Christian. Nguyen's wife, Chi Thi Nguyen (far left) searches through their family home to salvage what she could. Retired New York City firefighters John Seiler, (left photograph), and Chris Edwards, embrace after distributing relief supplies to survivors in Biloxi. The two were on duty in New York on Sept. 11, 2001, when terrorists crashed airliners into the World Trade Center. They decided to repay the kindness Americans showed New York by coming to South Mississippi as volunteers for the Red Cross.
JOHN C. FITZHUGH, DAVID PURDY

TEARS AND COMFORT

A Red Cross worker consoles Trahera Neely at a shelter in Bel-Aire School in Gulfport. Neely, who lived in Ashton Park apartments, lost all of her belongings. NICK OZA

Shelter for the homeless

Mary Garry waits in a shelter at Bel-Aire School in Gulfport with hundreds of others who lost their homes. Garry had moved to the Coast just a year before the storm. Nick Oza

COMFORT FROM THE SEA

The hospital ship USS Comfort arrives in the Port of Pascagoula to provide aid and emergency medical care. Akeem Pipes, a sailor stationed at Naval Station Pascagoula, helps secure mooring lines as the ship docked. AL DIAZ

THANKS, MIAMI

While her family searches through boxes, Raven Brooks, 6, brings a treat to her 1-year-old sister, Raelyn, from a pile of relief supplies sent from Miami, Fla., to Waveland. AL DIAZ

Supplies for Saucier

James Barnett (left) of the Saucier Fire and Rescue Department and other volunteers unload boxes of bottled water from a National Guard Chinook transport helicopter at Saucier Elementary School. The water was distributed at a relief station set up at the school. DAVID PURDY

The cash arrives

U. S. marshals countersign checks at the Red Cross check distribution site at the United Artists Biloxi 10 Theater parking lot. The site distributed several hundred checks a day to survivors. John C. Fitzhugh

COWBOY COOKIN'

Wayne Saur stirs up a large pot of homemade stew at a relief center in Gulfport. Saur and his friends, Wheeler and Lauren Hughes, loaded two trailers with food purchased with donations from folks in their hometown of Comfort, Texas, and left their ranch to spend a week camped out in front of Trinity United Methodist Church in Gulfport. The small group of real-life cowboys cooked food for relief workers and anyone else with a hankering for a hot meal prepared the old fashioned way - in iron pots over an open fire. CHRIS STANFIELD

A PRESIDENTIAL RESPONSE

President Bush talks to Joyce Rogers of Biloxi during his first visit to the devastated city. Rogers and her husband, Dennis, lost their home and most of their possessions. JOHN C. FITZHUGH

CHAPTER 4
MISSISSIPPI RISING

The Spirit of South Mississippi

Many of those who faced Katrina on Aug. 29, 2005, were the children and grandchildren of the storm of 1947, Betsy (1965) and Camille (1969).

By Stan Tiner
Executive Editor

Through the years, we have heard Camille survivors' tales of shared danger, of the heroes and the rebuilding efforts whose mortar was filled with sweat and tears.

So when Katrina passed, leaving our beautiful Mississippi Gulf Coast devastated with a 40-mile-long line of rubble containing dreams, landmarks and the bodies of many of our people, it was time to discover who we were – the inheritors of the Coast spirit.

But not all the inheritors recovering in Katrina's wake are native-born. They were drawn to the Coast because of its industrial base, military presence or to our casinos. That, in itself, helps to define the area's spirit. We are used to change. We are used to working with people of different backgrounds, walks of life, ethnicity. It's the variety of lives that help make us strong and ready for the task at hand.

But despite continuously being buffeted by the winds of change, Coastians often are said by newcomers and outsiders to be "some of the nicest people I've ever met." They wear a willing smile and are quick to offer a helpful hand.

'I fight for my life'

While cleaning the yard of her Biloxi home, Carmen Stepanek found an American flag that had washed up with the storm surge. Making reference to the "Karate Kid" movies, she pulled out a black bandana, placed it on her head and said, "I am Karate Mama. I fight. I fight for my life." She says she will not leave her home and will help rebuild her community.
James Edward Bates

And they were no different after Katrina wreaked destruction on a scale never before seen in the United States. When history books describe such events, Katrina will be among the three largest, with the other two being the San Francisco earthquake and the Great Chicago fire.

More than 68,700 homes were destroyed, and 65,000 more were heavily damaged. Almost no one's home or business in the coastal counties escaped intact, and the giant storm's destruction was visited well over 100 miles inland.

This massive blow has and is testing the will, character and spirit of our region like none other.

As the world watched, South Mississippians shook off the first days of shocked amazement at what Katrina had wrought, and gratefully accepted the assistance offered to us from a caring nation and those from beyond our shores. Then we stood tall, with much dignity and strength, and we went about the task of the rest of our lives – rebuilding lost homes, businesses, cities.

Our recovery is being forged one step at the time, one day at the time.

The flow of electricity was quicker for most than what could have been expected and Coast businesses figured out imaginative ways to get up and running on some level. Roads were rebuilt, debris removed and shelters closed.

A governor's commission, funded in part by the Knight Foundation and philanthropist Jim Barksdale, went to work, listening to residents' input on how they wanted their new South Mississippi to look. Scores of designers, planners, artists, architects, code specialists and others completed a whirlwind of meetings designed to help them envision 11 new cities.

Throughout all of this, the people of South Mississippi have dealt with unimaginable personal loss – both in terms of life and personal property. We have cried and hugged with our friends and family and fellow workers and we have become closer as a consequence of this shared pain. We have buried our dead and grieved for our collective loss even as we went about the business of rebuilding. Is that spirit? No, that is magnificent spirit.

Our task has just begun, but the lessons learned from those who came before us have been well learned. We know many of us will not see the beautiful rebuilt landscape of the future. But we know, too, that we will all have had a role in laying its foundation, and that our own spirit will become part of the legacy of the future.

That is who we are. We build and we rebuild, and the one constant through the generations is that spirit that cannot be defeated.

Not even by Katrina.

LOOKING TO THE FUTURE

At an editorial board meeting at the Sun Herald, publisher Ricky Mathews (right) listens to Gov. Haley Barbour as he discusses hurricane relief efforts. Mathews is one of four vice chairmen on the Governor's Commission for Recovery, Rebuilding and Renewal.
DREW TARTER

THANKFUL

"God bless you babies," Anita Averhart, 45, of Biloxi said to firefighters searching for survivors and bodies. Firefighters from around the country came to help the region. JARED LAZARUS

Can-do attitude

Mississippi Department of Transportation officer David West cheers up survivors as they stand in line at a FEMA ice and water distribution center in Biloxi. West said a positive attitude was important in getting through a disaster. JOHN C. FITZHUGH

GETTING IT DONE

Lew Beachy (left) and Joseph Miller of Lobelville, Tenn., cut a tree off the roof of a mobile home in Gulfport. The two were part of a crew of 11 men from the Believers in Christ church that came to South Mississippi to help. "We're just going where there is a need," said Beachy. "There's plenty to do." JOHN C. FITZHUGH

A TREASURE TO KEEP

Charlotte Williams of Long Beach, left, found her prized plate from Italy almost immediately upon first stepping into her destroyed home. The plate had fallen off the kitchen wall and made it out the back door to rest partly under the house without even a chip. Williams said the hand-painted plate was purchased at the Vietri showroom on a vacation to Italy. Michelle Allee, below, was able to salvage just a handful of her paintings. They had been for sale at Chessy's, a Bay St. Louis gallery. Allee, a professional artist, said she had about 45 paintings at the gallery. CHRIS OCHSNER

Leading men

President Bush, top right, flanked by Mississippi Gov. Haley Barbour (right) and Jim Barksdale, chairman of the Governor's Commission for Recovery, Rebuilding and Renewal, meets with business leaders and local officials in Gulfport. It was Bush's fifth visit to the region. David Purdy

Gulfport Mayor Brent Warr, above left, talks with a group of architects with the Mississippi Renewal Forum Commission near what is left of the harbor master's house in the Gulfport Small Craft Harbor. The commission, formed by the governor, was tasked with developing a master plan to rebuild South Mississippi. The visiting architects and city planners were divided into 11 groups and toured 11 cities. David Purdy

Former President Bill Clinton, left, meets with members of the Mississippi National Guard who lost their homes. Clinton came to Gulfport to discuss how the Bush-Clinton Katrina Fund should be spent. John C. Fitzhugh

WATER OF RENEWAL

Tom MacIntosh of the First Baptist Church of Gulfport baptizes his daughter, Connie, on the first Sunday after Katrina. His church, which was destroyed, and First Presbyterian Church of Gulfport held combined services at Crosspoint Community Church in Gulfport. JAMES EDWARD BATES

On the same page

Harrison County residents provided feedback on the proposals for redevelopment presented at the Mississippi Renewal Forum. The meeting was one of several that gave residents the opportunity to help direct their future. JOHN C. FITZHUGH

STICKING TO IT

There was an eager willingness among residents, like a family in Waveland, left, to rebuild after Hurricane Katrina. Throughout South Mississippi, signs of resiliency could be seen. Tractors tear away pieces of the imploded entertainment barge of Grand Casino in Gulfport, below, after it was washed onto U.S. 90. Officials expected to have the barge cut up and removed in two weeks. |John C. Fitzhugh

Rebuilding piece by piece

Jerry Hall salvages wood to patch the roof on his North Gulfport house. Residents became "weekend warriors" as they cleared yards, covered roofs and repaired their homes. John C. Fitzhugh

We're back!

Louis Pendarvis plays the trombone with the band Chez Mignonne on Main Street in Bay St. Louis. Vendors gathered for the first time since Katrina damaged the downtown area for Second Saturday, a sidewalk event featuring music, art and shopping. James Edward Bates

BUILDING UP

Gary Edgecomb (right) and Henry Heller lift the rafters for a pre-fab shed into place. The men were part of Building Goodness, a nonprofit organization that helps the needy. They were helping residents in Pearlington rebuild. DAVID PURDY

LOOK INTO THE FUTURE

Residents of Hancock County were given a look at the possibilities of their future communities at Our Lady of the Gulf Community Center in Bay St. Louis with the travelling Mississippi Renewal Forum.

SEEING THE NEED

Mississippi Gov. Haley Barbour and First Lady Marsha Barbour examine the damage in the Point Cadet community in Biloxi. Barbour joined an entourage with President George Bush, who visited the Gulf Coast several times to encourage residents. TIM ISBELL

SHARING HER STRENGTH

Marsha Barbour, wife of Gov. Haley Barbour, became one of the staunchest advocates for Coast relief, visiting the area numerous times to assess the needs. MARK CORNELISON

KATRINA COULDN'T STOP 'CAMP HOPE' FROM ROLLIN' PRESSES

By Stan Tiner

The front page of the Aug. 29 edition of the Sun Herald asked the poignant question: "Another Camille?" By mid-afternoon that day we knew the answer to the question – no, it was not another Camille; Katrina was many Camilles at once and the telling of this story would become the all-consuming story of our lives.

The Sun Herald had not missed a publication day in our 121-year history, and we would not miss publishing the Aug. 30 edition.

A handful of reporters remained in the newspaper building, just three blocks from water's edge but north of the protecting railroad tracks. The building sprang some significant leaks, but held firm against the mighty winds.

As soon as the storm had more or less passed, those of us who stayed along the Coast, and who were able to return to the building, did.

Meanwhile, a team of Knight Ridder editors, reporters and photographers pre-positioned in Montgomery were speeding to Biloxi to join us. They were armed with satellite phones, chainsaws and journalistic comradeship of the highest order. Our building was dark and the halls eerily lit with a bank of low lights when I saw Knight Ridder vice president Bryan Monroe and his intrepid band roll into the place we came to call "Camp Hope." The Marines had landed, and we were rolling together toward telling the story of the worst day in our history.

Communication was virtually non-existent – no cell phones, no land lines, no electricity. The Coast's infrastructure was gone. Major bridges linking us on U.S. 90 were washed away along with more than 68,700 homes. U.S. 90 itself no longer existed over great distances. Survivors wandered out of the shells of their homes, aimlessly drifting here and there asking for food and water.

It was an overwhelming scene.

Meanwhile, our reporters went where they could, one after the other returning to the newsroom to report that their own homes had been destroyed. We hugged them, cried with them and then went on with our task.

That Monday night, Biloxi Mayor A.J. Holloway came to the paper. He looked shell-shocked but brave. His aide, Vincent Creel, showed us an incredible video of the tidal surge roaring through Biloxi, past City Hall where they had stayed during Katrina. "This is our tsunami," the mayor told us.

That was our headline – 'Our tsunami,' on the eight-page newspaper we produced that first day after the hurricane in Columbus, where a team of Sun Herald editors and designers had gone ahead of Katrina. Twenty thousand copies were trucked in and delivered to shelters and wherever else Katrina survivors gathered.

Reporters and photographers on their way to cover the story across South Mississippi carried bundles of papers to distribute; for the first three weeks following Katrina, the newspapers were all free, even as we ramped up distribution to more than 80,000 a day, the highest circulation in Sun Herald history.

While there was great pride on the part of the Sun Herald that we had achieved our mission and published a newspaper on Aug. 30, it seemed, too, that our community felt a similar pride. Katrina had kicked our collective butts but somehow the newspaper had been printed. Holding the little paper, feeling it, seeing the pictures of devastation, showed them the Coast they could not see; this newspaper was tangible evidence that the local institutions were working and had not been defeated.

Meanwhile, our Web site was the primary link of information to the outside world. For many, our blogging throughout the storm and after, and solid updating through every day that followed, made us a viable part of the news produced from our home turf.

But the around-the-clock work effort and the stress produced by personal losses and the constant scenes of destruction took their toll. The shared pain of staff, including the dozens of news team volunteers, was palpable.

For the paper, and the community, we are a long way from normal but we are rebuilding and recovering together.

We would like to salute the Sun Herald staff – and that includes the many volunteers who brought their incomparable talents to our newsroom and became part of our team in every sense of the word. It was an honor to be associated with these journalists. The words, the images, the design have blended in the telling of an incredible story – one whose last chapter is far beyond our dim vision.

CAMP HOPE

Sun Herald staffers and journalists from other Knight Ridder newspapers worked from the Sun Herald offices in Gulfport, before, during and after the hurricane. Meetings were held twice daily to assign and select stories and photographs for the next day's paper. Discussing the page one photograph are (from left) photographer Patrick Schneider of the Charlotte Observer; Drew Tarter, photo director at the Sun Herald; Mike McQueen, managing editor of the Macon Telegraph; Stan Tiner, Sun Herald executive editor; and Bryan Monroe, vice president for news at Knight Ridder. NICK OZA